Original title:
Melancholy's Midnight Masquerade



Author: Juliana Wentworth
ISBN HARDBACK: 978-9916-90-682-8
ISBN PAPERBACK: 978-9916-90-683-5

## Secrets Between the Stars

In the night sky, whispers glow,
Dreams of ages, secrets flow.
Planets dance in cosmic grace,
Hiding stories in their trace.

Moonlight drapes the world in hush,
Gentle winds begin to rush.
Galaxies in silent sweep,
Hold the truths that we must keep.

Constellations weave a tale,
Of lost loves and ships that sail.
Wishes carried on a breeze,
Echo softly through the trees.

Stardust scattered, time stands still,
In these moments, hearts can fill.
With the magic, hope ignites,
Secrets shared on starry nights.

## Veiled Hearts Under the Night Sky

Under the stars, our dreams take flight,
Whispers of secrets in the cool night.
Veils of shadow, then bursts of light,
Hearts entwined, lost in the sight.

Gentle winds carry our sighs,
Echoes of love, under moonlit skies.
In this embrace, time softly flies,
Veiled hearts awaken to sweet goodbyes.

## The Longing of Shattered Reflections

In broken glass, I see your face,
A haunting trace in an empty space.
Whispers of love, a shadowed grace,
Shattered reflections find their place.

Every fragment tells our tale,
A love that dances, yet grows pale.
In the silence, my heart sets sail,
Longing for what we could unveil.

## Ribbons of Darkened Light

In the twilight, ribbons entwine,
A dance of shadows, a silent line.
Light flickers softly, hints of divine,
Darkened dreams in colors that shine.

Through the whispers of night's embrace,
We find solace in this sacred space.
Under the stars, hearts interlace,
Ribbons of light, a fleeting grace.

## A Serenade of Silent Tears

In the hush of night, soft tears fall,
Each drop a note, a silent call.
Melodies linger, memories recall,
A serenade whispers, enchanting all.

Through the quiet, our spirits soar,
A symphony played behind closed door.
In each heartbeat, emotions pour,
Silent tears, a love we adore.

## The Gossamer Gloom

Veils of mist around me creep,
Whispers of the shadows weep.
In the stillness, silence hums,
Echoes sway where darkness comes.

Threads of twilight softly twine,
Spinning tales of what's benign.
Glimmers fade in twilight's loom,
Trapped within this gossamer gloom.

## Midnight Chimes of Forgotten Dreams

Moonlight casts a silver trace,
Softly calling, time and space.
Chimes ring clear with stories past,
Seeping shadows, dreams amassed.

Echoes of a distant sigh,
Secrets that the night can’t lie.
Every bell tolls memory’s seam,
Midnight whispers of a dream.

## Elegy for a Lost Horizon

Once bright skies now cloak the day,
Colors bleed and drift away.
Fading light, a distant star,
Time's cruel hand, a vengeful scar.

In the dusk, we mourn the bright,
Yearning for that vanished light.
Once we soared, but now we roam,
Finding echoes of a home.

## The Ballad of Broken Masks

In a room where echoes lie,
Faces drift that never cry.
Masks adorn the hollowed face,
Hiding truths we can’t embrace.

Songs of laughter, tales of fear,
Silent screams that none can hear.
Time will strip the layers fast,
Unveil hearts beneath the masks.

## Shadows of Solitude in the Night

Beneath the stars, a silence lies,
Whispers of dreams, in moonlight rise.
Lonely paths where shadows play,
Embrace the night, let fears decay.

Soft echoes drift on autumn's breeze,
Crescent moon, a watchful tease.
In the stillness, hearts entwine,
Solitude sings, a song divine.

## Enigma of the Hallowed Night

Stars align in mystery,
Veiled secrets, history.
Night enfolds with gentle care,
Breath of magic fills the air.

Footsteps light on paths unknown,
Frozen moments, seeds are sown.
In shadows deep, the truth takes flight,
Embrace the enigma of the night.

## Echoes from the Hidden Realm

In the twilight, whispers call,
Echoes rise, they seem to fall.
Veils of dusk conceal the day,
Hidden realms where spirits play.

Rustling leaves, a tale retold,
Ancient secrets, brave and bold.
Every heartbeat, every sound,
Echoes of the lost surround.

## A Portrait in Dusk's Embrace

Dusk descends with a gentle grace,
Colors blend in warm embrace.
Brushstrokes bold, the sky ignites,
A portrait born of fading lights.

Golden hues kiss the horizon,
Nature's dreams in shades of reason.
Moments linger, time stands still,
In dusk's embrace, hearts are filled.

## A Masque of Grief and Joy

In shadows deep, the heart does weep,
Yet joy will bloom where sorrows creep.
A smile hidden behind the mask,
Both pain and laughter, a daunting task.

The echoes of laughter fill the air,
While tears fall soft in silent prayer.
Each moment a stitch in the fabric of time,
Inwoven threads, both bitter and sublime.

The dance of memories swirls like smoke,
Each whispering secret, a gentle poke.
For in the sorrow, joy does reside,
A symphony played on two sides, side by side.

Life's masquerade continues to spin,
A balance of both, we lose and win.
Within the heart, a tempest rages,
As love and loss write our stages.

## Dancers in the Gloom

In the whisper of night, shadows sway,
Figures emerge from the edge of gray.
With silence profound, they move like dreams,
Dancers in gloom, in chill moonbeams.

Footsteps echo where no light can tread,
In spectral robes that the lost have shed.
They twirl and glide on the edge of despair,
Whispers of longing fill the cool air.

In this twilight, hope flickers dim,
Yet still they dance, on a delicate whim.
Every movement tells a tale of the past,
Of love that was found, and shadows cast.

As dawn approaches, the figures disperse,
Leaving behind their delicate verse.
In our hearts, they linger, forever in bloom,
The dancers weave stories within the gloom.

## Veils of Fate and Longing

Behind each veil, a story lies,
Whispers of fate echo through the skies.
Threads of longing entwined with hope,
In tangled paths, we learn to cope.

Beneath the stars, where shadows play,
Dreams collide with the light of day.
Each veil a barrier, each sigh a breath,
In the silence of night, we ponder death.

Yet love persists in the softest hue,
A promise of dawn, the breaking anew.
With every tear, a lesson learned,
In the dance of time, our spirits burned.

So lift the veils, allow the light,
To guide us gently through the night.
With every heartbeat, we dare to find,
A thread of fate that is kind.

## Rhythms of the Unseen

In the hush of night, the whispers play,
Invisible rhythms guide our way.
With every heartbeat, the world does pulse,
In the fabric of life, we find our impulse.

The unseen dancers twirl in delight,
Casting their shadows in the moonlight.
Each step a story, each turn a chance,
A waltz of fate in a cosmic dance.

Beyond the veil of our weary sight,
Lives the essence of all that is right.
For in the silence, we hear the song,
Of love and loss, where we all belong.

As we journey forth, let us remain,
In rhythm with all, through joy and pain.
In the unseen, our spirits are free,
Dancing together, just you and me.

## **Melodies from the Abyss**

Whispers dance in the deep,
Echoes of dreams long gone,
A haunting tune that creeps,
From shadows where we belong.

Waves crash against the stone,
Through the darkness a song flows,
Calling the lost back home,
In a world that no one knows.

Stars shimmer, fading light,
A lullaby from the dark,
Guiding souls through the night,
To where hope ignites a spark.

In the depths, a heart beats,
Melodies lost in the sea,
Each note a tale that repeats,
Of who we used to be.

## Shadows of Longing Beneath the Stars

Underneath the silent sky,
Wishes drift on midnight air,
Dreams of the past float by,
In shadows we bare our despair.

Stars whisper tales of old,
Secrets shared beneath their gaze,
Longing hearts brave and bold,
In the night's gentle embrace.

Every moment swells with sighs,
As we chase the fading light,
In the darkness, truth lies,
Boundless as the endless night.

Yet hope flickers, faint but near,
In these shadows, love will bloom,
Through the silence, we will steer,
Together breaking through the gloom.

## Lullabies for the Lost

Softly now, the world sleeps,
Lullabies of the forgotten,
Close your eyes, take the leaps,
Into dreams where hope is begotten.

Winds carry tales on their wings,
Of those who wander far and wide,
In the silence, every song sings,
Of lost souls that once had pride.

Cradle them in softest light,
As the stars watch from above,
In the stillness of the night,
Let them feel our endless love.

For every sigh, a heartbeat,
In the tapestry of our tears,
Lullabies for the lost beat,
Rhythms calming all their fears.

## Where Secrets Sleep in Silence

In the hush of twilight's breath,
Secrets weave through the night,
Silent stories dance with death,
Unseen whispers take their flight.

Beneath the cloak of starlit skies,
Faded memories softly sigh,
In the stillness, truth implies,
That silence holds what we deny.

Underneath the ancient trees,
Buried dreams flutter and fade,
In the quiet, long to seize,
The echoes of the love we made.

Where shadows blend and linger on,
In the quietude, they creep,
Every promise, every dawn,
Is a secret we wish to keep.

## Whispers of a Forsaken Waltz

In twilight's hush, they once would spin,
Echoes soft, where love had been.
Hearts entwined in time's embrace,
Now but shadows in empty space.

A melody lost in forgotten air,
Faded whispers, a silent prayer.
Each step recalls the warmth of days,
Now only haunting, silent ways.

The moonlight drapes the empty floor,
Once a stage of longing lore.
As shadows dance in the cool night breeze,
Memories linger, refusing to freeze.

Yet still, the night recalls their song,
A tale of love, where none belong.
In dreams, they'll waltz 'neath starlit beams,
Forever trapped in forgotten dreams.

## Shadows Beneath the Velvet Veil

In twilight's grasp, the shadows creep,
Beneath the veil, where secrets sleep.
Whispers linger in dusky night,
Flickering flames, a fragile light.

The air is thick with tales untold,
Of hearts once brave, now quiet, cold.
Glimmers of truth in shadows reside,
Where hopes are nurtured, and fears confide.

Veils of midnight, soft and still,
Conceal the dreams that time can't kill.
Within their folds, lost wishes hide,
In quiet corners, where love once thrived.

Step lightly now, through shadows cast,
For every sigh may echo past.
In velvet gloom, the heartbeats race,
Finding solace in the hidden space.

## Echoes of a Silent Soiree

The rooms are dressed in moonlit grace,
Where laughter once filled every space.
Now, silence reigns with heavy sighs,
And every glance tells longing lies.

Crimson petals on the floor,
Remnants of joy now seen no more.
Echoes linger of sweet refrain,
In twilight's glow, in soft disdain.

Chandeliers flicker, a ghostly dance,
Where hopes once bloomed, now lost chance.
In every corner, memories play,
Of a vibrant night turned to gray.

Yet still, the night hums a tune,
As starlight drapes the fading room.
In silence, the heart seeks to replay,
The echoes whispered at the soiree.

## The Dance of Distant Dreams

Beneath the stars, a waltz unfolds,
In whispered dreams that time beholds.
Each note a step in dreams once bright,
Now safely tucked within the night.

Across the sky, the whispers glide,
Carried on winds, a timeless tide.
With every twirl, the heart does ache,
For dreams forgotten, paths we make.

In shadows cast by silver beams,
Echoes linger of distant dreams.
A dance of hope, of love's embrace,
In every sigh, we seek their grace.

Though far apart, they twirl and sway,
In realms where night enchants the day.
A timeless waltz in skies of blue,
Forever bound, in dreams made true.

## The Last Tango of Hallowed Souls

In shadows' dance, they drift and sway,
The whispers echo, night turns to day.
Each step a memory, a fleeting chance,
In the twilight's embrace, they find their romance.

Soft moonlight wraps their ethereal forms,
Two lovers spinning, amidst the storms.
Their hearts beat gently, lost in the sound,
Of timeless rhythms that know no bound.

The floorboards creak with tales of old,
While stars above in silence behold.
With every twirl, a promise is made,
As shadows linger, their doubts allayed.

In hallowed realms, where spirits tread,
Their souls entwined, where dreams are fed.
The last tango whispers, of love and loss,
In the quiet dusk, they bear their cross.

## Faded Reflections in Starlit Waters

In the still of night, where the echoes play,
Faded reflections shimmer and sway.
Stars dip their toes in the mirrored lake,
While secrets of whispers in silence wake.

The moon spills silver on the gentle tide,
Carrying dreams where shadows hide.
Ripples cascade, erasing the past,
As fleeting moments slip away fast.

Soft breezes carry a haunting song,
A lullaby where the lost belong.
In starlit waters, hearts intertwine,
Each wave a promise, a love divine.

As dawn approaches, colors collide,
Faded reflections begin to divide.
Yet in their depths, memories shine bright,
Guiding lost souls through the infinite night.

## Invitations to a Dusk-Draped Divan

Beneath the boughs, where shadows blend,
Soft whispers beckon, as daylight ends.
Cushions of velvet and softest sighs,
Await the secrets under painted skies.

With fingers entwined, they gather near,
Soothing the worries, quelling the fear.
A sanctuary of comfort, music's embrace,
Where every heartbeat finds its place.

Golden hues spill on the dusk-draped scene,
Invitations linger, sweet and serene.
Stories unravel with each gentle touch,
In this cherished haven, they cherish so much.

As twilight dances upon the floor,
The invitation lingers, longing for more.
With laughter and memories etched in the air,
Dusk holds them close, a tender affair.

## The Lament of Luminous Strangers

In moonlit glades where lost souls tread,
Luminous strangers seek dreams long dead.
Bound by their yearning, they wander alone,
In the night’s silence, their hearts made of stone.

Whispers of hope trail like fading light,
Each step taken in the depths of night.
With eyes like galaxies, they search the skies,
For the warmth of connection, where true solace lies.

Echoes of laughter entwine with the dark,
Fleeting reflections, like firefly spark.
Yet shadows linger, the past clings tight,
As strangers unite in the sorrowed light.

In the lament, they find a new song,
For luminous hearts can never go wrong.
Together they'll rise, through the pain and the strife,
Breathing in love, they reclaim their life.

## The Gloom Beneath the Gaze

In the depths of silence, shadows creep,
Whispers of sorrow, secrets keep.
Eyes that wander, lost in despair,
Searching for solace, finding none there.

Beneath a veil of twilight's hue,
Lies a heart that once knew true.
But hope grows dim, like fading light,
In the gloom that cloaks the night.

A distant echo of laughter fades,
Tangled in the sorrows that invade.
Each moment heavy with a sigh,
Under the weight of the unspoken cry.

Yet through the darkness, a flicker glows,
A gentle reminder, as the starlight flows.
For even in shadows, a path can be traced,
To find the warmth of a love embraced.

## A Dance Among the Shadows

In twilight's embrace, shadows sway,
Whirling softly, night meets day.
With every turn, mystery calls,
Echoing softly through ancient halls.

The moonlight glistens on forgotten dreams,
A silent witness to the world's soft schemes.
Footsteps whisper in the cool night air,
As spirits twirl without a care.

Each movement tells a story lost,
In the dance of time, we pay the cost.
Yet laughter echoes in the dark,
A fleeting moment, a tiny spark.

With every heartbeat, the night grows old,
A dance of passion that won't be told.
But in the shadows, we find our grace,
A timeless waltz in an endless space.

## Flickering Flames of Solitude

In the quiet night, embers glow,
A flickering warmth in the depths of woe.
Each flame whispers tales of the past,
Of dreams and hopes that didn't last.

The solitude wraps like a familiar cloak,
A gentle embrace that stirs and evokes.
Yet in the ashes, new life begins,
A testament to the strength within.

Beneath the stars, the heart beats lone,
In the flicker of fire, a truth is shown.
For even in darkness, light can arise,
From the depths of silence, hope never dies.

So let the flames dance in the night,
Igniting the soul with their steadfast light.
In solitude's cradle, wisdom is found,
As flickering flames weave a peace profound.

## Echoes of an Unheard Lullaby

In the stillness of twilight, a song unfolds,
An unheard lullaby, in whispers it holds.
Carried by breezes, soft and serene,
It weaves through the shadows, a gentle sheen.

Lost in the silence, the heart starts to yearn,
For melodies sweet that the night will return.
Each note a promise, an echo of grace,
Resonating softly in this quiet space.

Beneath the stars, dreams softly entwine,
In the echoes of whispers, the heart will align.
With every heartbeat, the lullaby flows,
Awakening feelings that no one else knows.

So let the night cradle these murmurs of love,
As the echoing lullaby wafts from above.
In the realm of the unseen, beauty takes flight,
Through echoes of dreams that color the night.

## Chasing the Phantoms of Tomorrow

In the haze of dawn's bright glow,
We chase the dreams we barely know.
Fleeting whispers on the breeze,
Guiding us through endless trees.

Futures crafted from a sigh,
Moments fleeting, passing by.
Each shadow dances, hopes anew,
In the twilight, we pursue.

Echoes ring from paths not taken,
In our hearts, a fire awakened.
With every step, we forge the way,
Chasing phantoms come what may.

Stars align in whispered fate,
As we run through time's own gate.
Tomorrow's arms are open wide,
With restless hearts, we will not hide.

## A Wisp of Dusk's Memory

The sun dips low, a crimson hue,
A wisp of dusk bids night adieu.
Memories linger in the air,
Soft as silk, without a care.

Whispers dance on evening's breath,
Tales of love, of life, of death.
In fading light, we glimpse our past,
Moments precious, too short to last.

Stars awaken, one by one,
Shadows stretch as day is done.
A quiet tune, the night will weave,
A gentle sorrow hard to leave.

Hold this eve in heart and mind,
In dusk's embrace, the truth we find.
For every wisp of memory dear,
Unraveled threads still draw us near.

## The Haunting of Wandering Hearts

In quiet rooms where echoes dwell,
Wandering hearts have tales to tell.
Each corner holds a haunting glance,
With shadows waltzing, lost in trance.

Footsteps soft on ancient floors,
Time dissolves behind closed doors.
With every sigh, our fates entwine,
In whispered dreams, our paths align.

A fleeting glance, a lover's plea,
In every space, sweet memory.
Though journeys take us far apart,
The haunting lingers in the heart.

Through the nights, through endless days,
We find our way in myriad ways.
For though we roam, we are not lost,
Wandering hearts pay any cost.

## The Dance of Shadows and Light

In the twilight where shadows blend,
Light and dark begin to mend.
A ballet fierce, yet soft and sweet,
A cosmic dance where spirits meet.

Flickers caught in golden rays,
Illuminating love's warm ways.
With every turn, the night ignites,
The beauty found in hidden sights.

Step by step, we ebb and flow,
In this rhythm, our spirits grow.
For in the dance, we find our grace,
In every shadow, we embrace.

As dawn breaks, we'll hold it tight,
The dance of shadows, purest light.
Together, we will make our mark,
In harmony, from light to dark.

## Portraits of Despair Beneath the Stars

In shadows deep, the quiet sighs,
Memories linger, where hope lies.
Stars weep softly, in the night,
Painting hearts with ghostly light.

Whispers travel on the breeze,
Carrying tales of broken trees.
Silent cries in the vast expanse,
Lost souls yearning for one last chance.

Each twinkle tells of dreams undone,
A lullaby for the weary one.
In their glow, secrets unfold,
Echoes of a kindred soul.

Yet from darkness, sparks may rise,
To kindle hope in midnight skies.
Within despair, the heart can heal,
Finding strength in wounds conceal.

## A Night of Longing and Dreams

Beneath a veil of silver light,
Whispers stir the tranquil night.
Hearts entwined with hopes unseen,
In between the spaces, we dream.

Echoes of love drift softly near,
Carried by winds we long to hear.
In shadows cast by the glowing moon,
Longing dances to a gentle tune.

Stars awaken tales of the past,
Moments fleeting, too quick to last.
A night so rich with whispered sighs,
Awakens courage in longing eyes.

As dreams take flight on wings of air,
The world feels lighter, free from care.
In silence, we seek what's true,
A night of longing, just me and you.

## Moonbeams and Memories

Softly the moonbeams touch the ground,
Whispers of nights where dreams abound.
Memories wrapped in silver glow,
In the stillness, hearts overflow.

Laughter echoes in the quiet time,
Moments woven like nursery rhyme.
Each beam a reminder of what was near,
Fleeting shadows, both sweet and dear.

Beneath the stars, we find our way,
Guided by light at the close of day.
Captured moments in the night sky,
Bring forth a tear, yet make us fly.

In the embrace of dusk's soft sigh,
We hold our memories, never shy.
Moonbeams dance, in a lover's grace,
Painting our dreams in a soft embrace.

## The Silent Symphony of Dusk

As day gives way to evening's breath,
A symphony plays, hinting death.
Silent notes drift on the air,
A curtain falls, a quiet fare.

Crickets sing in the fading light,
Nature's chorus bids goodnight.
Shadows stretch across the ground,
In their embrace, peace is found.

The sky transforms to vibrant hues,
A canvas brushed with twilight views.
Each whisper carried on the breeze,
Hints of magic among the trees.

In this silence, the world will pause,
Listening close, without a cause.
The dusk unfolds its gentle grace,
In the stillness, our hearts embrace.

**A Portrait of Light's Departure**

The sun dips low in violet skies,
Casting shadows where silence lies.
Each ray a memory left to fade,
In twilight's arms, a dream is laid.

Fleeting hues of gold and red,
Mark the path where daylight bled.
As night ascends with gentle grace,
It steals the warmth from daylight's face.

Whispers of dusk like softest sighs,
Paint the world as darkness flies.
A canvas brushed with fervent care,
Hold close the light, though it's not there.

So let the stars awaken bright,
To cradle dreams lost in the night.
For every loss, a beacon's glow,
A promise found in shadows' flow.

## The Phantom's Elegance Unveiled

A dance of veils in moonlit halls,
Echoing past where sorrow calls.
The phantom drapes in silver mist,
With elegance, a haunting twist.

Ghostly whispers through the night,
Weave a tale of lost delight.
In shadows deep, her gaze does roam,
A fleeting spirit far from home.

Veiled in silence, she takes her flight,
Through haunted dreams, a mystic sight.
Each step a note in time's refrain,
A sorrowed waltz, a sweet disdain.

Yet in the dark, there blooms a light,
A glimpse of warmth from endless night.
The phantom dances, still, she thrives,
In realms where only memory survives.

## Twilight’s Elegy for Lost Innocence

In twilight's haze, the laughter fades,
A chime of joy in shadows laid.
Children's dreams lost to the night,
As innocence takes its flight.

The stars like tears in heaven’s quilt,
Mark the path where love was spilt.
A gentle breeze stirs sorrowed hearts,
And whispers tales of broken parts.

Time drips slowly, a fading song,
With every note, we feel the wrong.
Yet in the dusk, a spark may rise,
To cradle hope within our sighs.

A fragile fire, a cherished glow,
Embraces us when shadows grow.
For even lost, the light remains,
In twilight’s arms, hope gently gains.

## In the Arms of Forgotten Whispers

Beneath the stars, where secrets sleep,
In hushed tones, the night doth creep.
Whispers linger like autumn leaves,
In the stillness where memory weaves.

Echoes call from the depths of time,
Soft melodies, lost in rhyme.
Each breath a sigh, a story spun,
Of dreams entwined, of battles won.

In shadows deep, the past unfolds,
Wrapped in warmth that silence holds.
Forgotten tales of joy and pain,
In whispers soft like gentle rain.

Hold tight the silence, let it flow,
For in stillness, the heart will know.
In every secret, love persists,
Embraced gently by whispered trysts.

## Somber Melodies in the Moonlight

The moon drapes shadows on the ground,
Whispers of long-lost dreams abound.
Soft melodies weave through the night,
Carried on the wings of fading light.

A lone owl calls from a distant tree,
Echoing sorrow, wild and free.
Stars twinkle like tears in the sky,
As the world below lets out a sigh.

Each note a story of love once bright,
Now wrapped in melancholy's bite.
The breeze carries secrets, old and worn,
In the silence of a heart forlorn.

Yet in this gloom, there’s beauty to find,
A dance of shadows, gentle and kind.
For within the sorrow, a spark may glow,
Illuminating paths we often forego.

## A Ballad for the Brokenhearted

In the still of the night, a heartache sings,
Lost in the web of shattered things.
Tears like raindrops fall to the ground,
Each one a memory, forever unbound.

The echoes of laughter now bittersweet,
Filling the spaces where love once would meet.
Hope dances lightly, on the edge of despair,
Fleeting like whispers in the chilly air.

Days drift like clouds in a somber sky,
Time twists and turns as the moments pass by.
Yet in this sorrow, a lesson remains,
In the art of love, joy sometimes wanes.

So pen down your grief, let the ink flow free,
Finding solace in words, your heart's decree.
For tender ballads can mend a soul,
In the embrace of music, we can feel whole.

## The Enigmatic Veil of Night

The stars are shrouded, behind a dark veil,
Whispers of magic in the night's tale.
Shadows and dreams meld into one,
Under the watch of the midnight sun.

Mysteries linger in the cool night air,
Secrets entwined in the moon's soft glare.
The world transforms in the stillness of dusk,
Pellets of hope buried deep in the husk.

Soft winds carry stories, untold and strange,
Fables of fantasy that seldom rearrange.
Wanderers roam, with hearts open wide,
Seeking the wonders that true night can provide.

Yet safety lies wrapped in the cloak of the dark,
A sanctuary found in each quiet spark.
For in the enigma of the night's embrace,
We discover our shadows and find our place.

## A Dancer's Solitary Reverie

In a dim-lit room, where silence reigns,
A dancer twirls, free of chains.
Her movements paint stories in the air,
Expression of longing, a soul laid bare.

Feet whisper softly on the wooden floor,
Inventions of grace from a heart that yearns more.
Each spin a reflection of dreams she keeps,
A blend of joy and sorrow that gently seeps.

Alone in the spotlight, shadows grow tall,
Yet she embraces them, answering their call.
With each gentle sway, a tale unfolds,
Of love and loss, of whispers and bolds.

The music concludes, but the dance won't cease,
For within her spirit, there’s everlasting peace.
In solitude's grip, she finds her release,
A dancer resplendent, a dreamer at ease.

## Portrait of a Heart in Mourning

In the quiet corners of my soul,
Where memories cling like shadows,
A heavy heart, it takes its toll,
Lost in the depths of time's meadows.

Each tear reflects a whispered name,
Echoes of laughter now turned to sighs,
Love's warmth, once a fervent flame,
Now flickers softly, as daylight dies.

Silhouettes dance on walls of grey,
Framed by the dusk of shattered dreams,
Yearning for words we failed to say,
Caught in the web of love's lost seams.

Yet in this sorrow, hope remains,
A promise wrapped in time's embrace,
For every heart that feels such pain,
Will someday find its sacred place.

## The Enchanted Abyss

Beyond the veil where shadows dwell,
Whispers of magic beckon me,
In the depths of a timeless spell,
Where wishes float like leaves on sea.

The stars above, they weave a tale,
Of dreams that shimmer, soft and bright,
An ocean deep, where spirits sail,
Guiding lost souls through the night.

With every wave, a secret shared,
A dance of fate on azure waves,
In this abyss, I find I'm dared,
To dive beneath, where the heart braves.

In the currents, truths collide,
Awakening the dormant past,
In the dark, my fears subside,
For in the abyss, I'm free at last.

## The Forgotten Waltz of Shadows

Underneath the moon's soft sigh,
Two silhouettes begin to sway,
A haunting waltz where whispers lie,
In the forgotten night's decay.

They twirl through halls of faded grace,
Where echoes of a laughter linger,
A tender touch, a fleeting trace,
As time slips through a phantom finger.

The music plays, a distant chime,
Guiding them through silvered fear,
In the shadows lost to time,
They dance in dreams, forever near.

Yet with each step, the dawn draws nigh,
A bittersweet farewell to keep,
As shadows fade, their spirits fly,
Into the arms of endless sleep.

## Chasing the Ghosts of What Once Was

In the haze of forgotten dreams,
I roam through echoes of the past,
Chasing whispers, silent screams,
Fragments of joy that couldn't last.

Through winding paths of memory's haze,
I seek the moments lost in time,
Illicit laughter, forgotten days,
Wrapped in the dusk of what was mine.

But shadows linger, teasing fate,
With every laugh, a twinge of pain,
In this pursuit, I hesitate,
Bound by the ghosts that still remain.

Yet still I run, for hope is bright,
A spark that guides me through the dark,
In chasing ghosts, I find my light,
Reviving dreams that leave a mark.

## Cloaked in Nuances of Gray

Clouds drift softly above our heads,
Veiling the light in shades of dread.
Whispers of silence float through the air,
In every corner, a tale of despair.

Grays whisper secrets, tales untold,
In faded dreams, where hearts grow cold.
Hues blend softly, a muted sound,
In the stillness, our sorrows abound.

A canvas painted with weary hands,
Shades of regret, where hope never stands.
Life's palette mixed with shades of ache,
In this silence, we're bound to break.

Yet in the gray, small sparks ignite,
A flicker of warmth, a glimmer of light.
Cloaked in shadows, we find our way,
In the whispers, we learn to stay.

## A Serenade for the Sorrows

Sing softly, my heart, through the night,
For sorrows wrapped in fleeting light.
Each tear that glistens, a memory shared,
In the echoes of laughter, we're sometimes ensnared.

Notes carry whispers of grief so deep,
In the corners of dreams where shadows creep.
Melodies linger, sweet yet forlorn,
A dance of the lost, forever reborn.

Underneath moonlight, hearts conspire,
Each note a flicker, a fleeting fire.
Together we'll sway through the depths of pain,
In the melody's arms, we're free once again.

So let us embrace this serenade,
In the symphony of life, no truth will fade.
For every sorrow sings a song,
In the chorus of dusk, we all belong.

## Illusions Woven in Shadows

Beneath the veil of a starlit sky,
Illusions dance, and dreams whisper by.
Shapes in the dark, they flicker and fade,
In the realm of shadows, our fears are laid.

Threads of silver, in darkness entwined,
Woven through stories that linger in mind.
Every heartbeat tells what we fear,
In the tapestry of night, we draw near.

Illusions bloom like flowers at dusk,
Fleeting in beauty, shrouded in husk.
Glimmers of hope in the corners we find,
Woven with sorrows, by fate intertwined.

In this theater, illusions may reign,
Yet amidst the chaos, we gather our gain.
For every shadow gives rise to light,
In the depths of the night, we emerge bright.

## The Unseen Guests of Gloom

In the corners lurk the unseen guests,
Whispers of shadows, uninvited quests.
With silent footsteps, they tread the room,
Bringing their tales of undying gloom.

Echoes of laughter fade into the night,
As flickering candles dim their light.
Each guest a memory, wrapped tight in time,
In the fabric of life, they gently chime.

Haunting the halls with their weighty sighs,
Unseen companions in sorrow's disguise.
Together we linger, no words to impart,
The gloom gathers softly, binding the heart.

Yet in their presence, we find the way,
Through valleys of shadows, we learn to stay.
For every unseen guest bears a truth,
In the depths of despair, there lies our youth.

**Unraveled Threads in Time**

A tapestry woven fine,
Each thread a story told.
Fingers trace the years that bind,
Secrets in the folds unfold.

Memory dances in the light,
Whispers of a bygone hour.
Every stitch a fleeting sight,
Time drips like a fragile flower.

Moments flutter, drift away,
Echoes linger in the air.
Unraveled threads, the price we pay,
For lives entwined beyond compare.

Through the fabric, shadows play,
Warp and weft, a soul's embrace.
In the night, the dreams betray,
The beauty of the human race.

## When Shadows Converse

In the twilight, secrets blend,
Shadows stretch and start to speak.
Whispers of what minds transcend,
Echoes soft, yet bittersweet.

Beneath the stars, lost tales emerge,
Silent voices in the dark.
A symphony begins to surge,
Finding solace in the stark.

As twilight drapes the world in grey,
The past and present intertwine.
In the stillness, spirits play,
Time's embrace, so undefined.

When shadows converse, truths align,
In the quiet, hearts unmask.
Unseen threads that softly twine,
Revealing what we dare not ask.

## Specters at the Edge of Dawn

With the dusk, they start to rise,
Echoes of the night take flight.
Faint reflections in the skies,
Specters dance just out of sight.

In the hush, their stories flow,
Carried on the morning breeze.
Whispered tales of long ago,
Floating softly through the trees.

As dawn unfurls its golden hue,
Memories linger, hearts respond.
Chasing shadows, we pursue,
The phantoms of a bond we've donned.

At the edge of day's embrace,
Time stands still in softest grace.
Specters greet the sun's warm face,
As dreams awaken, a warm trace.

## Vestiges of the Faded Past

In corners dark where memories hide,
Vestiges of love remain.
Faded photographs reside,
Echoing our joy and pain.

Dusty shelves of yesteryears,
Lingering scents of time long spent.
Fragments soaked in laughter, tears,
Whispers of intent still rent.

Worn-out books with fragile spines,
Pages turning slow and soft.
In their words, a world entwines,
Carrying the dreams aloft.

The past, a tapestry unspooled,
Yet in each thread, a lesson cast.
In shadows of the life once ruled,
We find ourselves through echoes vast.

## Secrets in the Twilight

Whispers dance on the evening breeze,
Hidden thoughts blend with ancient trees.
Shadows play where the light holds sway,
Promises made at the close of day.

Footsteps follow a path unseen,
In the hush, where the heart leans.
Glimmers of hope in a fading light,
Secrets bloom in the quiet night.

## Moonlit Sorrow and Starlit Secrets

Beneath the glow of a silver sphere,
Sorrow lingers, yet dreams draw near.
Each star twinkles with tales untold,
Memories wrapped in the night's soft fold.

The moon weeps for what has been lost,
While shadows remind us of the cost.
In the silence, hearts intertwine,
With whispered secrets that love confined.

**A Waltz with the Weeping Willow**

Gentle sway of the willow's tears,
As the night falls, it calms our fears.
Branches reach like arms to embrace,
In its shadow, we find our place.

A waltz begins with the rustling leaves,
Soft notes drifting as the heart believes.
Together lost in the dance of time,
Moments cherished in rhythm and rhyme.

## When Time Stood Still in the Dark

Silence fell like a velvet shroud,
In the dark, dreams lingered proud.
Moments stretched like a golden thread,
In stillness, the heart dared to tread.

Whispers echo through the void of night,
Fleeting shadows come into sight.
With time suspended, emotions flow,
In the dark, we let love grow.

## Revelry in the Regretful Hours

In twilight's haze, we dance and swirl,
Each laughter masked, each heart a whirl.
The shadows whisper secrets dear,
While lost hopes linger, sharp and clear.

We toast to dreams that slipped away,
With fleeting joy, we dare to play.
Yet in our smiles, a hint of pain,
A joyful mask hides subtle strain.

In the corners, echoes softly sigh,
Of sleepless nights and questions why.
The music fades, the truth unwinds,
In revelry, our sorrow finds.

Yet here we twirl in fleeting bliss,
Embracing warmth, a fleeting kiss.
We hold onto this fragile hour,
In revelry, we find our power.

## Shrouded in Elegance and Grief

The gown whispers tales of silent woe,
Adorned with diamonds, a fragile glow.
Each stitch a memory caught in time,
A dance between the sublime and crime.

The candlelight flickers with despair,
Illuminating shadows of silent prayer.
In elegance worn, the heart beats slow,
A fragile mask hides the aching below.

Draped in sorrow, yet poised with grace,
In every glance, a haunting trace.
The world moves on, but we stand still,
In the chasm of loss, we seek to fill.

So let the night embrace the tears,
In elegance, we confront our fears.
With every breath, we rise anew,
Shrouded in grief, yet the beauty grew.

## The Gaze of the Uninvited

On cobbled streets, where shadows blend,
A lonely figure, a heart to mend.
They watch the laughter from afar,
With longing eyes like a distant star.

The laughter spills, a joyous sound,
In circles bright where hopes abound.
Yet one untouched, they stand alone,
A ghostly presence in a world not known.

Each smile they see, a bitter strain,
The warmth of fellowship feels like pain.
They yearn to join, but stay apart,
The uninvited with a heavy heart.

Yet in that gaze, a quiet strength,
A story woven through time and length.
In solitude, they find their way,
The uninvited, in shadows, stay.

## Veils of Longing and Remorse

Beneath the moon’s soft, silken light,
Veils of longing dance through the night.
With each gentle breeze that sweeps the land,
A quiet ache, a sorrowed hand.

Whispers of dreams in the cool night air,
Memories linger, a heavy stare.
In the folds of fabric, stories reside,
Veils of remorse where feelings hide.

A soft caress of what was lost,
In the reflective silence, we count the cost.
Each flicker of hope, a fragile thread,
Woven with wishes from words unsaid.

Yet in the twilight, we dare to seek,
Through veils of shadows, our hearts speak.
In longing’s grip, we find our way,
Embracing remorse, we live, we sway.

## Masks of Solitude and Sorrow

In shadows cast by waning light,
Silent tears embrace the night.
With weary souls, we hide our face,
Behind a mask of cold disgrace.

Each smile a fragile, fleeting guise,
A fragile truth beneath the lies.
In quiet corners, whispers grow,
As lonely hearts begin to sow.

Among the echoes of despair,
We wander lost, with dreams laid bare.
But in this silence, hope may bloom,
As love breaks through the heavy gloom.

So let us shed these masks we wear,
And face the world with hearts laid bare.
For in our scars, we find the light,
That guides us through the endless night.

## A Gloomy Gala at Twilight

The chandeliers gleam with distant flares,
Yet in their glow, a thick fog stares.
Dressed in shadows, we sway and glide,
With heavy hearts and secrets inside.

Laughter dances on the chilling breeze,
While voices whisper, pleading, 'please.'
A masquerade hides our burdened truth,
As dreams decay, stolen by youth.

The clock strikes slow, each second drains,
While echoes linger in ghostly chains.
In this dark ball, we search for light,
But twilight cloaks our fragile plight.

Yet beyond the veil of somber art,
Hope flickers faintly in every heart.
As dawn approaches, the shadows flee,
Revealing the strength of you and me.

## Secrets Behind the Hushed Facade

Behind closed doors, the stories dwell,
In whispers soft, we weave our spell.
The paint may peel, the shadows creep,
Yet in these corners, memories sleep.

Facades worn thin, they softly crack,
Revealing truths we can't take back.
In quiet moments, our ghosts arise,
Each secret held beneath the guise.

With every smile, a tale untold,
In shattered dreams, the heart lies cold.
Yet in the dark, we find a way,
To share our burdens come what may.

So let us lift this heavy weight,
In honest hearts, we find our fate.
For in the light, we come alive,
With every truth, we learn to thrive.

## The Veiled Heart's Lament

In twilight hours, the heart does ache,
Burdened by choices, fragile and fake.
A love that flickered, then turned to dust,
Lost in a whisper, betrayed by trust.

Behind the veil, the heartbeats mourn,
For dreams that faded, souls forlorn.
Each tear a treasure, a silent plea,
A lament woven in memories.

The echoes linger, a haunting tune,
As shadows stretch beneath the moon.
In grief, we gather, our sorrows sing,
Binding us close to the pain they bring.

Yet in this sorrow, there lies a spark,
A hope that flickers within the dark.
For even veiled, the heart will yearn,
To love again, to rise, to learn.

## An Overture of Lost Souls

In shadows deep, where echoes play,
The whispers of the night convey.
Forgotten dreams flicker and fade,
Guiding us through the twilight shade.

With every sigh, a tale unfolds,
Of heart's desires, of secrets told.
In silent cries, the truth emerges,
From longing hearts, the pain surges.

A symphony of spirits lost,
In search of light, they bear the cost.
Through haunted paths, they roam alone,
Yearning for a place called home.

Beneath the stars, they dance and weave,
In realms of dreams, they dare believe.
An overture of souls in flight,
A haunting song through endless night.

## Midnight's Hidden Lament

Beneath the cloak of midnight's hue,
Where shadows blend with dreams anew.
A silent tear falls to the ground,
For whispered hopes that can't be found.

The moonlight weaves a silver thread,
Through silent prayers of words unsaid.
In aching hearts, the echoes swell,
Each sorrow tells a tale to tell.

In the stillness, a voice will rise,
From depths of night, beneath the skies.
Lamenting for the days gone by,
As fleeting moments softly sigh.

Midnight's breath brings forth the pain,
A haunting melody of the rain.
Yet in the dark, a glimmer shines,
A hope that weaves through midnight's lines.

## The Dance of the Wandering Spirits

In twilight hues, the spirits play,
They swirl like leaves in fall's bouquet.
With laughter light, they drift and glide,
In dances bold, they will not hide.

Through ancient woods, their laughter sings,
A melody of forgotten things.
Each step they take, a story spun,
Of battles lost, and victories won.

They beckon forth with ghostly hands,
To realms unseen in shadowed lands.
In every corner, their traces remain,
A fleeting glimpse of joy and pain.

The dance goes on beneath the stars,
With secrets shared, both near and far.
A mingling of the past and now,
As wandering spirits take their bow.

## A Tapestry of Forgotten Whispers

Threads of time weave tales untold,
In patterns rich, both bright and bold.
A tapestry of whispers gone,
Beneath the sun, they linger on.

Each stitch a memory, soft and light,
Of laughter shared and hearts in flight.
In shadows deep, the stories fold,
A chronicle of life retold.

Weaving through the fabric's seam,
A silent echo of a dream.
With every thread, a soul entwined,
In the fabric of those left behind.

A tapestry of whispers spun,
Where echoes dance and shadows run.
In faded colors, the past aligns,
As time's embrace forever binds.

## Reflections in a Glass of Teardrops

In the stillness, droplets form,
Each a memory, a hidden storm.
They shimmer softly in the light,
Pieces of sorrow, captured tight.

A mirror's truth, bare and bright,
Each tear tells tales of lost delight.
In their depths, a world confined,
Stories of love, and hearts entwined.

Dark clouds gather, shadows creep,
In a glass, the secrets keep.
Reflecting back what once was real,
A fragile heart, a fragile seal.

But in the drops, hope finds a way,
To mend the wounds of yesterday.
With every tear, a lesson learned,
In the glass of tears, hope is burned.

## A Nocturnal Reverie of Regret

Under the moon's soft, watchful eye,
Echoes whisper, and memories sigh.
Once vibrant dreams, now shrouded in gray,
Charm of the night steals breath away.

In shadows long, regret takes form,
A tempest fierce, a raging storm.
Forgotten wishes, like whispers fade,
Promises broken, deep debts unpaid.

Stars bear witness to silent cries,
As ghosts of thought in darkness rise.
Each fleeting moment, a fragile thread,
Weaving the paths that we once tread.

Yet night shall pass, a dawn will break,
In light we find the strength to wake.
To mend the hearts, to heal the pain,
And dance in light, where hope remains.

## Shadows Dance at the Witching Hour

When midnight sings its haunting tune,
The shadows dance beneath the moon.
Whispers swirl, a ghostly sigh,
As secrets seep from lips nearby.

Figures waver on cobblestone,
In twilight's grip, they drift alone.
Each shadow tells of tales untold,
Of love and loss, both fierce and bold.

In the silence, fears entwine,
As spirits beckon, hands align.
In the fleeting, dim-lit hour,
Lies the truth of lost power.

But dawn will break and chase away,
The shadows dancing in dismay.
A new beginning shall arise,
To reforge dreams and cast new ties.

## Whispers Beneath a Silver Veil

Beneath the veil of silver light,
Soft whispers float into the night.
Secrets shared in hushed refrain,
Emotions dance, like gentle rain.

Each word a thread, a bond so dear,
Sewn with memories, laced with fear.
In the twilight, emotions bloom,
While the shadows chase away the gloom.

Hearts unmasked, laid bare and true,
In the calm, where dreams renew.
Voices linger, soft and low,
In the embrace of the night's flow.

Yet as dawn breaks, whispers fade,
And truth becomes the heart's upgrade.
Beneath the veil, life intertwines,
In every whisper, the love redefines.

## The Acolyte’s Autumn Dream

Leaves whisper secrets, drifting down,
The sky wears hues of burnt orange crown.
In shadows deep, where spirits roam,
An acolyte wanders, seeking home.

Beneath the ancient oak, whispers call,
Starlit wishes wrapped in twilight's thrall.
Promises of change in every breath,
In autumn's chill, finds solace or death.

Crimson sunsets bathe the weary ground,
Where echoes of laughter and sorrow abound.
The rustle of branches, a soft refrain,
In the heart of autumn, beauty and pain.

As daylight fades, a new path unfurls,
An acolyte's journey through leaf-strewn swirls.
With every step, the dream intertwines,
In the tapestry of fate, the heart defines.

## Masquerade of Unspoken Words

In shadows cast by flickering light,
Masked souls dance through the velvet night.
Behind the silk, true selves concealed,
Emotions clash, yet none revealed.

Whispers float like petals on the breeze,
Promises linger with delicate ease.
A glance, a gesture, hearts out of sync,
In the silence, all thoughts lost in ink.

Masks crafted with care hide truth's embrace,
Each sigh a step in this fleeting race.
Through the chaos, a yearning grows strong,
A melody played where the silent belong.

When the evening wanes, and masks must fall,
Will the heart speak, or remain small?
In this masquerade, will we be free,
To share the words of our deepest plea?

## Withered Roses at Twilight

Petals fall like memories lost,
Each withered rose bears the weight of cost.
Twilight drapes the garden with woe,
Where love once bloomed, now shadows grow.

Among the thorns, a whisper remains,
Of laughter once shared, now muted pains.
In the silence, echoes of sweet perfume,
Fading away in the encroaching gloom.

Beneath the boughs where the dusk light dims,
A heart remembers the songs and hymns.
Yet time creeps on with relentless stride,
And even the fairest petals must hide.

As stars awaken in the darkening sky,
Withered roses teach us to sigh.
For in every ending, a new dawn waits,
In the garden of life, love never fades.

## Shimmering Mirage of Sorrow

Across the desert, dreams take flight,
A shimmering mirage etched in twilight.
Illusions dance on the shifting sand,
Promises made by an unseen hand.

Lost in the vastness, a heart aches slow,
Chasing reflections that only shadows know.
Each step a burden, every breath a plea,
In the landscape of longing, yearning to be free.

Beneath the starlit sky, hope flickers dim,
A lone traveler searches as daylight grows grim.
What lies beyond the horizon's bend?
A gift of solace, or sorrow's end?

Yet through the mirage, truth finds a way,
Emerging at dawn to brighten the day.
In the heart of despair, resilience will rise,
For hope is the light that never truly dies.

## Ballad of the Subdued Heart

In whispers soft, the shadows creep,
A tender heart, its secrets keep.
The moonlight casts a gentle glow,
On dreams that dance, but never show.

Through quiet sighs, the echoes breathe,
Of love subdued, yet still believe.
With every beat, a silent plea,
That yearns for more, yet longs to be.

A melody of hope persists,
In corners where the darkness twists.
Though voices fade, and hopes may part,
A ballad born from a subdued heart.

Yet in the night, a spark remains,
A light that flickers through the pains.
In solemn grace, the heart will rise,
To seek the dawn, to claim the skies.

## Haunting Melodies of the Night

In shadows wrapped, where secrets dwell,
A haunting sound begins to swell.
The night unfolds its velvet arms,
And lures the heart with fragile charms.

A whisper soft, like distant drums,
Through empty streets, the echo hums.
Each note a ghost, from days long past,
In moonlit dance, they hold us fast.

Beneath the stars, where sorrows blend,
These melodies never seem to end.
In every chord, a story spun,
Of love once lost, of battles won.

So listen close, for in the air,
The night imparts its gentle care.
In haunting melodies that sigh,
The soul finds peace, beneath the sky.

## The Last Dance of Heartstrings

In twilight's glow, the moment stays,
A final dance in soft arrays.
With every step, the heartstrings sway,
To melodies that drift away.

A partner lost, yet spirits near,
Through whispered dreams, they draw us clear.
With every twirl, a tear may fall,
In echoes of a love's last call.

Each heartbeat marks a cherished time,
The rhythm plays a soft, sweet chime.
In fragile light, the shadows pass,
As memories in silence last.

So let the music guide the night,
To where the heart finds purest light.
In every spin, a story gleams,
The last dance holds our fleeting dreams.

## Secrets Linger in the Dark

In corners deep where shadows dwell,
Lie whispered truths, too shy to tell.
The night conceals, yet beckons near,
As secrets linger, ever clear.

Through hidden paths, a silence grows,
Unraveling tales that nobody knows.
Each breath a shiver, each glance a clue,
In the stillness, the heart beats true.

Among the stars, where wishes hide,
The darkness wraps the dreams inside.
Yet flickers of light may pierce the veil,
As hearts unveil what shadows trail.

So tread with care, in muted grace,
For in the dark, we find our place.
In secrets held, our spirits spark,
Embracing all that lingers in the dark.

**Masquerade of Distant Echoes**

Whispers dance in twilight's arms,
Voices weave through shadowed charms.
In the night, the colors blend,
Life's a game with no clear end.

Faces fade in the twilight's glow,
Secrets linger in the flow.
Fragments of laughter fill the air,
A masquerade, a fleeting flare.

Time slips by with silent grace,
Each heartbeat a hidden trace.
Masks conceal the truth inside,
In this realm where dreams abide.

We twirl in the echoing haze,
Caught within the swirling maze.
Yet behind each sly disguise,
Hope shines brightly in our eyes.

## The Veil Between Regret and Hope

A curtain drawn, a sigh released,
In longing hearts, regrets increased.
Yet hope's light flickers in the dark,
Where shadows fade, igniting a spark.

Memories cling like morning dew,
Whispers lost, yet feelings true.
Between the lines of joy and pain,
A bridge is built through every rain.

The past may haunt with silent cries,
But future calls beneath the skies.
In twilight hours, the heart can mend,
Finding solace, the soul ascends.

Through the veil, we cautiously tread,
Hesitant steps where angels tread.
In this limbo, we seek the light,
Regret's embrace transforms to flight.

## Lament of the Lonesome Moon

Beneath the stars, she weeps alone,
Her silvery tears, a sorrowed tone.
In stillness, she watches lovers sigh,
While shadows dance, and dreams pass by.

A witness to the fleeting night,
Her glow a balm, soft and bright.
Yet deep within her aching core,
A longing heart forever sore.

Each phase she shifts, yet still feels lost,
In emptiness, she pays the cost.
Her light a guide for weary souls,
Yet hidden in her silent tolls.

Waltzing through the star-kissed skies,
She cradles wishes wrapped in lies.
The lonesome moon, forever true,
Whispers love to the night's soft hue.

## Cloaked in Yesterday's Sorrows

A shadowed past, it clings to me,
In whispered tones, it longs to be free.
Memories drape like faded gold,
Tales of warmth that once were told.

Echoes of laughter, now bittersweet,
With every step, I feel defeat.
Yet in the pain, a lesson lies,
Through tears that fall, the spirit flies.

Cloaked in burdens, I rise anew,
Transforming sorrow, I chase the blue.
In every heartache, strength is found,
A melody where hope resounds.

Today's dawn breaks the heavy chains,
Weathered skies give way to rains.
Through every shadow, a light will shine,
Cloaked in the past, I learn to find.

Milton Keynes UK
Ingram Content Group UK Ltd.
UKHW021952151124
451186UK00007B/194

9 789916 906828